Fighting with Angels, Dancing with Devils: The Poetry Collection.

By John Davies.

COPYWRITE JOHN DAVIES 2018 ©

All rights reserved. No part of this publication may be reproduced or transmitted in any form or by any means without permission of the author of the individual work.

Books by John Davies.

King of the Sunset Strip Volume One: Poetry & Lyric Collection.

King of the Sunset Strip Volume Two.

Black Paradise Society: Poems from an Insane Mind.

Stood up by The Devil: The Poetry Collection.

Fighting with Angels, Dancing with Devils: The Poetry Collection.

"Dedicated to Clinton, Wayne & Spencer Davies. I am fortunate to see another year, but without you. I will live life the way you'd want me too. I will keep you three remembered. I will keep you proud of me. Until we meet again boys".

John Davies 14/10/2018.

She looked like
She was worth a million
Dollars, but you could
Tell that she was just
Another wannabe
Sunset Queen.
She had sores around
Her mouth and smelt
Like last night's bar action.
She was never going to
Find the right punter.
She was death in a glass.
She glanced back
As she walked in front
Of the rail car.
We could all see this happening
Yet nobody cared enough
To save her.

It was quite on the
Sunset Strip and the
Kings had returned home
To take back what was
Rightfully theirs.
A year away from running
The sidewalks
They were a sore sight
For some but an immediate
Threat to others.
The warning signs came out.
There was going to be
A war with no witnesses
To the killings.

Some of us speed
Through life while
Others stay in the
First lane and inevitably
Get taken over at
The first opportunity.
It is the decision
Of the individual
To stay in the traffic
And watch life
Pass them by.

It was supposed to be
A reunion of minds
But the minor irritation
That you always fed me
Shone through immediately.
I sat there listening
to your stories and current
successes in life
and in the end when
I finally got the chance
To say two words
Only two came to mind.
Good evening!
I stood up and left
Through the nearest door.
Bar right. The smell
Of your fake aftershave
And cheap suit dulled
Any opinion and was eventually
The last memory that
I ever had of you.
I walked home disappointed
In myself. I should have
Stayed at home.

Trust always amazes me
As it is like a reputation.
Takes a lifetime to earn
And only takes seconds
For someone to destroy.

She watched you
From the shadows
Already plotting your demise.
She was the Black
Magic Lady. She was the Devil
In disguise.

The more I thought
About you the more
I realized that I should
Have let you go sooner.
I was being selfish as usual
And expecting you to
Watch my back forever.
It was the moment that
I dropped my guard
That you struck.
It was a low blow
But nothing more than I
Expected from someone
Like you.

Teachers stand in front
Of a desk with a white board
And a tablet. The kids these days
Can do their homework
On an iPad. They use Google
To get the answers to their
Homework. In the old days
We had to trawl for hours
Through text books and

Encyclopedias.
This scares me as the next
Generation of kids after
This one won't be made to
Attend schools or universities.
They will be allowed to sit on their
Asses having virtual lessons
And cheating their way to
Perfect scores via the internet.
They will leave school
Feeling intelligent when in actual
Fact, all they have done
Is surf the internet.
Reality bites and their first
Day in their first jobs will be
An absolute eye opener.
And the poor tax payer
Will once again be supporting
Their sorry asses while they
Tap away again to feel
Like they've had a career.
Roll on their retirement. The streets
Will be littered with brainless
Zombies with twitchy thumbs.

Frozen hands that
Reflected her heart.
The Ice Queen was waiting
For you in the dark.
She showed you a smile
She blew you a kiss
And the last thing you'll know
Is the last thing you'll miss.

I had to make
A decision on whether
I was going to leave
A place I enjoyed
Or carry on getting
Abused by a manager
Who only saw flaws
In me and called me
High maintenance.
He had his favourites
And once upon a time
I was the top of the list.
Christmas ended and he got
His bonus along with
The fools that followed him.
I missed out by two months.
It would have cleared
All of my credit card bills.
At my age I needed stability
Both for myself
And my family.
Instead, I wake up to
Stupid messages, thinly vailed
Threats and the impending
Need to start looking for
Another job. This is the rewards
For being the hardest working
Manager in the building.
I became a threat.
I had to leave.

We've met so many
Along the way and yet
Don't really know
Them at all.

I know so many strong
Women and am proud
To have more female friends
Than male. It's all about
The testosterone and
One up man ship with men.
Women don't really care
Who you are and what
You do. It's all about where
You are going and the route
You need to take to complete
That journey. It's not about
Feeling more comfortable
In their company. It's just
Nice not to be competing
All the time and trying to get
The last word in.

God gave me a voice
But I decided
To write it all down
Instead. It made more
Sense to me that way.
It gave me something
I could understand.

The snow fall was heavy
This year. March 2018
Was immense. Woke up to the
Beauty of a Christmas time
Scene but the trains were
Cancelled. Snow on the tracks.
The roads were icy
And I ended up in a car crash
That saw me head first
Into a tree. It was a blast.
It really was.

People with talent
Champion those
Who try.
People without talent
Take to social media
To try and destroy
Those who are trying
To perfect their art.

Pizza at midnight.
Cold Viognier wine.
Blueberries and a TV show
About fast, cool cars.
I should be in bed
But the mind is still
Winding down.
Watching a film with
Popcorn and smoked bacon
Right now would be
Awesome. A blue daquiri
And my PJ's. Some jelly beans.
Today almost went badly.
Confronted by a fellow manager
With no right to wear the badge.
I almost lost it. I sit down now
In reflection. I was so close
To losing my job today
And he was so close to losing
His two front teeth.
Not anyone gonna replace them
For Christmas either.
You need a pay cheque for that
And the little idiot
At only 23 years of age
Is now on his 3rd redundancy.
Like a cat on it's 9th life.
Time to find something you are

Actually good at kid
Instead of annoying
People who'd chew you up
And spit you out
Like the bad taste you are.
I hope we never meet again.
It could end up
Very bad for you.

We get to middle age
And decide to go
On a health trip.
We eat sensible.
Drink sensible. Exercise.
It's as if we are trying
To prolong a process
That is inevitable.
This journey has no
Time limit. It has no respect
For time either. It always
Takes. From day one we
Are racing against time.
We grow older. The lines
Appear around our eyes.
Our eyes fade with time
And from the sights
They have seen.
Both good and bad.
Our skin wrinkles.
We grow wiser with age
And our outlook becomes
Different from when we were
Younger as we know that
Our time is getting shorter.
Yet we always retain
The child within us always.

There is a fear
That the nostalgia
Could become syrupy
And that what we once
Loved many years back
Will turn into just
Another novelty act
Never to be enjoyed
In the same way again.
We watch our former Icons
Dancing around on the stage
With a tired act and barely
Unrecognizable voices
Beaten by too many concerts
And too much fast life
When they once were relevant.
A while back I use to do the
Retro tours until it got too
Painful to watch some of the
Acts crawl through their set
And barely make it past the
Finish line. I think the best
Way to be remembered
Is by leaving when your time
Has come to an end. It saves the
Reputation from being tarnished.
You get to retire at the very
Top of your game and not
Be some sad hanger on
Looking for the next dollar
And photo opportunity.
Signing autographs for people
Who didn't remember you
Your first time around
But want a selfie with a 'famous' name.

Desire is like
An old street car
With a burning vapor
And the devil inside
It's shell. Racing towards you
Like a death in a quite
Back alley. Nobody to notice.
Nobody will ever care.
Only the track marks
Will be seen once they've
Run over you and left you
Bleeding at the scene
Of the crash.

We turn scenarios
Over and over
In our minds
And never come
To a peaceful
Conclusion.
We analyse everything
Yet never come up
With any answers.
We feel utterly
And desperately alone
And we turn to those
Who's smile we though
Was a comfort
But in reality was a frown.
We can't keep on
Doing this to each other.
There will always be
A loser when the rules
Are breached.

I barely noticed you
Looking in my direction
Because you were looking
Backwards and I am always
Looking into the future.

I always wanted
To be the star
Of an Andy Warhol
Canvas. I wanted to
Hang with all of the
Cool cats listening to
Lou Reed and the Velvet
Underground & The Doors.
Hanging around with people
Like Jim Morrison, Nico
And Ultra Violet.
Drinking in a bar like
The Moloko Vellocet
From a Clockwork Orange.
I always wanted to stand out
And hang with the cool kids
At school. It was only natural
That this need would continue
Well into my adulthood.
And now middle aged
With children of my own
I am hoping to pass on the
Baton. To make them
Experience what I did
When I was once of an age
That they will one day be.
It's not a need to live through
Them but more for them to
Enjoy something they will never
Experience in their own lifetimes.
Classic Cult movies without a big budget.

The best thing
About the past
Is that it ended
This morning.

I drank your favourite
Wine and it reminded
Me of you. I could taste
Pears, oils and citrus
Fruits and it bounced
Off my tongue like a kiss
Goodnight. Falaghina grapes.
The hills of Benevento.
A place I've never seen before
But can imagine seafood
And moonlights and laughter
With amazing friends.
My friend looked like
A china doll. Hardly aged
From birth. We could drink
This wine together and read
Poetry. I asked for her secret.
She smiled and walked away.
She had my attention.
I settled the bill and left.

Wanted to cook rustic chicken
For dinner tonight.
Wanted to finish my Aleister Crowley book.
Wanted red wine but white
Is better as it's cold.
Wanted the rain to stop
So I could finish the garden.
Wanted my son to cuddle up
On the sofa with me.
Wanted to find a better job
But no time to look for one.

Wanted to blast out Gary Numan
Songs and Kraftwerk
But the baby was asleep.
Then I looked at the bigger picture
As all some people want
In this world is fresh water
And something to eat.
A roof under their heads
And to feel wanted. Loved.
I felt selfish as I already had
More than I deserved in life
Yet took it for granted
As usual.

I dress well
I dress retro
Von Dutch
Judas Sinned
Voss belts (I got 7).
I'm a collector
A narrator
An Author (not awful though)
I have my very own
Internet troll.
Still a thousand places
That I'd love to go to.
I'm a father
Now an older brother
To one.
A poet.
A show off.
Hopefully a best friend
To a few of you.
I'm a paradox
The King of the Sunset Strip.
Most importantly
I'm alive.

And that's got to count
For something
I guess.

Oceans absorb us
And swallow us whole.
We are totally unaware
Of it's danger
Or of it's beauty.
We could be swimming
One moment
And the next
Drowning and ready
To become a tasty
Morsel for a predator.
Ironic. We eat small fish.
We re easily eaten
By their larger relatives.
The circle of live
Once again showing us
How vulnerable
We really are.
Drowned by the beauty
Of being free while
Looking for Mermaids
To fall in love with and
Save us as we drown.

Once again
I found myself
Looking for a way out
Of this place.
The world stopped
Feeling like home
To me and its inhabitants
Constantly working
Against me.

It got to the point
Where I had decided
To leave and find
Another path to follow
As the one I was
Previously on was no
Yellow brick road
And there was no rainbow
To follow either.

The realisation
That one day
I will be no more
Worries me
As I long to be free
But not from the
Ones who love me.
Only the reality
That I will no longer
See my family
And that I won't
Be around to see
Their successes
And achievements
In life.

We gelled together.
We became one person.
Almost. I found myself
Hopelessly and emotionally
Bound to you
Like a drug habit
I would never kick.
You would be
The final addiction
That would eventually
Kill me.

I chose you
Even before our
Paths crossed one
Another. It was a
Natural coming
Together of minds.
We just didn't
Know it at the time.
How were we to know
Then that we'd spend
The rest of our lives
As one.

We learn at an
Incredible rate.
Our minds absorb
Data and new
Information
Which we keep
With us until
The day we die.
We are the most
Powerful computer
System in the world.
When we die
Where does it all go.
Flown back into
The ether I guess.
Borrowed knowledge
On borrowed time.
We close our eyes
Finally after a long life
And our hard drives
Are deleted.

What will we be
Many years on
From now.
The future scares me.
I worry about
My children
And what will be
Left for them
After I've gone.
We were meant to
Enjoy being adults.
Now look at us
And what we've become.
Some of us
Never stood a chance.

I smelt your Izzy Miyake
In the air.
Heard your laughter
Through the airwaves.
In the bath
I was freezing cold
Yet, I felt you by my side
My motivation was gone
Yet you pulled me through.
Pushed me out of the door
To do it all again.
To get me through
Another day.
Though the music was sad
It bought you back to me
If only for that moment.
That short while.
Asleep forever
With that dimple in your cheeks
And yet it only seemed
Like yesterday when

The world moved on.
Stars fall from the skies
Yet Brother you'll always be
The one I will idolize.

Legends
Icons
Models
Supermodels
Los Angeles
Superstars
All have my books.
Wanna meet one
Of my American friends
Who can elevate me.
Didn't think so?
After all,
I'm writing books
You're selling looks
But nobody is listening.
Guess I gotta do this
On my own again.

You looked so peaceful
In your death sleep.
You were here with me
Still, but no longer
With me. The dialogue
Was over, for now.
Your appearance hit me
The most. Instantly changed.
Ghoulish. You became
Something I didn't know
In an instant. Within seconds
Of your last breath.
You went from existence
To a memory. This hurt me

The most as I wasn't ready
To say goodbye. It just
Wasn't in the script and
I handled it badly.
I never recovered.
I guess I never will.

Crystal chapel
And a Nun in a rage
We shot a bible
To the moon
Onto that higher stage
Baby, ride it down
Resident evil
Did I let you know
The friends that you reap
Are the crops that you sew
Baby, ride it down
Head held up
Like a pelican high
I got a 16th volume
Of a lullaby
Baby, ride it down
Optimum venue
With a pane of glass
There's champagne
In one hand
In in the other
Is her ass
You couldn't get much firmer
Just like a sculpture
With class
She took the easy
Way out as candles
Burn out way too fast
Baby, you got shot down.
Baby, you're no longer around.

We see shadows
In the dark and every
Corner poses its own threat
To our survival.
We chased a dream
And made a deal
With the Devil.
The centre of our
Universe collapsed
Immediately and we ran
To Angels who turned
Their backs on us.
We got exactly what
We deserved.
Nothing more.
Nothing less.

I sat alone in a taxi
Watching the world fly by.
70 mph and still not
At my destination.
Then again at this stage
Of my life I wasn't really
Sure if I had one anymore.
The rain poured down
And all I could see
Was the fluorescent glow
Of street lamps and headlights
Coming my way.
Travelling into the abyss
And Death awaited me.
She had a look on her face
That I mistook for a smile.

The world was drowning
All around me
And all that I had
To save me was
An umbrella
And a bottle of water.
Ironic that I was
Now drinking the one
Thing I had around me
In abundance
And the weight
Of it all swept over me
Like a tidal wave.

I had to make a choice.
I was in a conundrum.
I was in a death grip
And the addiction was winning.
The problem with people
Without the addiction
Is that they stare blindly
At those who are silently
Crying out for the help
They know they will
Never receive. It's a lost
Cause and it finally breaks you.

I long to make cherry
Moonshine with all
The hillbillies and eat a
32oz steak while dancing
Around a 12 foot tall
Campfire at midnight
Reciting Aliester Crowley
With the moonlight
Smiling down on me.
That would be swell.

My induction into Hell.
As all of us Devils laugh
Together.

Being lost
Is a scary feeling
When you once
Owned the map
To help you find
Your way home.

The Angel man
Went down smiling
Like the cool remnant
Of a childhood dream.
Serpents smiling
And wandering Gods
Searching for another way
To find their way
Back in. The town villain.
The loser, the drunk.
We sat by the harbor.
Small Italian village.
Drinking Grappa. Eating
Tomatoes and basil in olive
Oil and balsamic vinegar
With hard bread. Olives.
The smell and the swell
Of the tide under our noses.
The latitude. Salt air.
Young ladies on the menu
And the fishing boats
Clinging on to dear life.
I hear the sounds from the
Sea and a Mermaid
Called Destiny
Sings to me.

I
Hate
My
Terrible
Face.
My ugly
Face.
It dies
With me
And is
Gone
Forever.

All the young
Contenders make me
Realise that my time
Is not up for quite a while.
You see, for as long as it
Takes them to post
A picture and post
Four or five short lines
Then call that a poem
I've actually published
A full page of poetry
For my next book.
One that will once again
Feature worldwide.
But for now I will use
Them as my muses.
They feed me material.
I drink wine and I listen
To Jim Morrison singing
About lighting his fire
While I eat popcorn
And light a scented candle.

We were a slave
To the machine
And for as long as we
Accepted that we were
Always doomed
To live that lie
And continue with
A bleak outlook
For the future.
With no direction
At all. We lived each day
Like it was our last
Because that was all
We were ever taught.
It was all we ever knew.

We pouted and made
Stupid faces as if
Our lives would never end.
We posted the perfect
Pictures to friends
Who we would never meet.
We called it social media
Yet it was never social
And it never hit the mainstream.
We got a few likes
A few thumbs up's
But eventually everybody
Soon gets bored of seeing
Thousands of pictures
Of that same face
Over and over again.
They switch the light off
As they exist stage right
And move onto their next subject.

She breaks your heart
And then exits
The scene of the crime
With a smile
And a wave goodbye.
A silent gesture
That reduced you to tears.
She had Angel wings
But dived straight into Hell.

You made sure that
The insecurities about
The person you were
Translated to everyone
That you met in order
To drop them down
To your level.
You felt threatened
By the stronger members
Of your team, therefore
You took them off
The team sheet and
Relegated them to the bench.

She breaks your heart
And then exits
The scene of the crime
With a smile
And a wave goodbye.
A silent gesture
That reduced you to tears.
She had Angel wings
But dived straight into Hell.

Just look what we've
Done to this world.
Drained every resource
Available. Killed off species
To the point of existence
For tusks. Ivory. Greed.
The black market.
Everybody profits from
The cruel death of
An innocent animal.
Apart from the animal
Of course. A cowardly
Trophy seeker hidden
Behind a gun and then
Posting a picture with a
Proud look and a smile
On their smug faces.
No guilt for killing an
Innocent wild animal.
It has become more about
Mass production and
Giant corporations.
We no longer function
As Human Beings anymore.

I tried to make sense
Of it all but you were
The catalyst of everything
Bad that was happening
In my life at the time.
It felt like the walls
Were constantly closing
In on me and the feeling
Of claustrophobia was
Crushing me from the inside.
Making it hard to breath
And even harder to stay alive

In this prison cell world of yours.
I looked at flashing images
Of my past and many times
I felt ashamed. Many times
I felt proud. I needed to make
More memories with better
People. And to find the key
To this iron door that
You called your heart.

You kept your distance
But always had me
In your sight.
The demon seed
You injected in me
That darkness
In my life.
I looked in on life
From the outside
I watched you plunge
Your knife. It went deep inside
And severed me wide
My heart stripped bare of strife.

He called himself a poet
Even carried a little
Moleskin notebook around
With him. And every opportunity
He had, he'd get his quill pen
Out and write about the stars
At night. And the birds in the sky
And then tell everyone that
One day he would write a book
Be a famous author
And sign his name in them.
They found him late one night
Curled up on a park bench

With only an empty bottle
A sleeping bag and his little notebook.
Inside were blank pages
And under the same stars
He claimed to write under
He fell asleep forever.
Emptied into the void while still
Dreaming of infamy.

A hot bath
And silence
With just the cats
For company
And a scented candle
Is the perfect environment
To write poetry
On a Sunday morning.
Later I'll take the boys
And parents out for lunch
Somewhere nice and enjoy
A Mohito and dream
About a happy ending.
But for now the water cools
The soap suds are receding
And I need to find a towel.
There is much to do today
And I want to see
My hometown one last time.

A hard rain fell
Washing away all memories
And evidence
And as the killer looked
Out from behind the window
Now older yet none
The wiser and alone
He sees out the last few years

Of a life less ordinary.
Feeding a bourbon habit
While the fire crackles brightly
In the background.
Never caught. Never pained
By the life he left behind.
Never to be seen again.

You were a figment
Of my imagination
That I would only see
In my dreams.
Then people wondered
Why I always wanted
To sleep the days away.
If only to be with you forever.

I wasn't prepared
To give myself up
Completely.
There was still
A part of myself
That I wanted to
Hold onto.
There was a hope
Inside of me that
I could still be
John Davies again.
I work hard
And I deserve not
To be a franchise.
How I long
To be me again.

We pour our hearts
Onto a blank page
And expect people
To dilute those words.
We live the memories
That we become happy to
Finally share with the
World. It gives us release.
The art is the disease
Inside us that we share
With the whole world
Until finally, we lease that stage.

We were beautiful disasters
Life's outcasts.
We waited always
At the back of the queue
For we deemed ourselves
Not worthy of standing
In line with the rest
Of humanity. We were
Conflicted. Desolate and
Self loathed. We were the class
Of 1975 and were suppose
To be in the prime of our lives.
Instead, worn out by life
We just wanted anomynity
And a quite corner to rest
Our glass and dream of the past.

Our evolution is a
Testament of the person
We aspire to be.
Whereas the correlation
Between the people that we
Once were to what we once
Tried is a very different concept.

We follow leaders who in their
Own version of life have got it
Wrong beyond repair but
Are propelled to greatness
By the media owned by
Corporations and politicians
Who buy the votes.
The cable television shows
What they want us to watch.
We buy stuff we don't need
To impress people we don't even like.
This is 2018. The year of
The iPhone zombie
And everyone looks great
Staring down into a phone.

We fall out of contact
And touch with one another
Yet always find our way back
To one another.
Everything's eventual.
Time spins wildly
Out of control and as we
Grown older we finally
Understand the reality
Of our ever decreasing time here.
So we try and achieve
As many things as possible
So that by the end of our lives
We can say that it had
All been worth while.

There are no road maps
In Hell. Only the Hell that you
Experience when you finally
Arrive at your final destination
With a puzzled expression on your face.

I see myself
When I look into the
Faces of my two young boys.
Only their innocence
And beauty truly
Captures the fact that
We are actually so much
Different from one another.
They can light up a room
While my soul only collects
Dust and attracts the dark.
Maybe this is why I suffocate
Them with the love that I do.
I'm scared of letting them
Loose into the world and
Becoming tainted by the whole
Ugliness of it all.

I saw you differently
Yet you never
Saw me at all.
I was invisible.
A ghost.
I was nothing
Yet you were
My everything.

You left your tears
On my pillow as a
Subtle reminder that
Would haunt me forever.
They turned cold
To the touch and dried
Quickly. I knew then that
Was the last physical contact
I would ever have from you
Ever again. That was

Your parting gift to me.

You took the very worst
Of me and turned
It into something amazing.
For every negative
You saw a positive
And used the magic
Inside of you to change
The darkness inside of me.
You gave me a fresh hope
A maturation in my life
And each day I never
Say thank you. Maybe it's the
Narcissist in me. The self loathing
Ogre. The clown. The joker.
Maybe I take life for granted
When we are surrounded
By others who deserve it more.
Maybe I shouldn't think so much
As it normally gets me in trouble.

I've spent years
Convincing myself that
I was never good enough
And there became a small
Battle deep within me
To push myself to the limit
On a daily basis. As a young man
It worked, but as I grow older
Maintaining the balance
Gets tougher every day.
You see, it's the pride
Of the old warrior who never
Wans to feel decline or defeat
But we age and with that
At some stage we need to lower

The expectations we set ourselves.
We could cash and burn so easily
When all we needed to do
Was drop down a gear
And extend our time here.
We are not machines.
Our children deserve more than that.

I wish I lived
In a different time
When friendship was true
And love was divine
I wish that everything
Felt sublime
As I was yours
And you were mine
And every sentence
That we spoke
Was true romantics
No joke
And make up took us
Back to our youth
Without the internet
When we had to
Tell the truth.

We worship animal gods
And take in the diseased air
In which they lay.
We are sentenced to live
This way forever while
The world decays all around us.
We saw this as an easier way
Out of here. We were blinded
And in hindsight never regained
Control of ourselves again.

You were shrouded
In mystery and mystique.
You wore a shawl that
Covered most of your face
And all I saw was almond
Coloured eyes that sparkled
Like the stars in a lithium sky.
We had a backdrop of sand dunes
And the laughter of old men
Telling older stories while
Cooking over a hole in the floor.
Thank you Marrakesh.
I dined in the side streets
Drinking rose water and got
Drunk from the welcome I received.
It was a beautiful time
Yet time continuously passed me by
Yet you walked straight passed me
And all I'll remember is your eyes.

We entered into a friendship
That had many quirks
But was so much more
Different to anything
I had ever experienced before.
I was a straight man
You were a married gay man.
We lived in two very different
Worlds yet somehow it worked
In a strangely bizarre way
That you became my children's
Godfather and also a best friend.
Somewhere along the line
We sat in a gay bar in Soho
Drinking cocktails and discussing
Christmas and life in general.
I felt relaxed and proud.

Happy that I've given my Sons
A life lesson in acceptance.
But next time we meet up dude
The Tequila is on you.

I was shot out of the womb
One day back in 1975
When the world was a completely
Different place to where
It is today. Almost 43 years later
I am the surviving brother.
There were three of us.
The other two lost along the way
As well as a half brother.
I am alone yet feel the love
From strangers I will probably
Never meet. They give me strength.
They give me hope.
The deal is that they don't know me
So owe me nothing.
However we connected and
I'd be lost without the light
They shine in my direction.
We were never meant to
Live alone as Human Beings.
Always meant to copulate
With one another. We make choices
With who we side with. I chose well.

I always wonder
What a 50 year old me
Will look like
When the current
42 year old me
Looks so terrible.

In our quest we usually
Have to suffer many defeats
Before we can raise ourselves
Back to our feet again.
It is normal. It is everyday life.
But be nice to those people
Who you collude with on
Your way up as they will
Still be there waiting for you
On your way down.
Be humble. Appreciative of
Your surroundings as one day
It could all be over and then
You're the one standing
At the bottom of that ladder
Looking up as live passes you by.

I sat down with you
At 9pm one evening.
The winter chill
Had set in. You had a small
Dog that you wrapped
Inside a small blanket
While you wrapped your
Arms around yourself
And prayed that you'd
Make it through to the
Next morning. It was
Christmas Eve. I'd just finished
A 13 hour shift. I saw you
From the corner of my eye
Watching happy, laughing
Couples walk past you
As if you were invisible.
Human trash to be thrown
Out with the recycling.
I also walked past you.

The difference was to walk
Into the shop you were
Sitting outside. I bought you
A hot coffee. Food. Dog food
And a bottle of red wine.
It didn't change your
Christmas Day the next morning
But you were still somebodies
Child, and as a Father
I just couldn't walk past you both.

You became a walking
Meth lab on legs.
An amphetamine whore
Who skipped through life
And fell through doors
And no saving grace
Could ever hide the trace
Of that little girl inside
Lost and distant out in space.
You had blown up lips
That could no longer kiss
And the smell of cheap perfume
I would no longer miss
And the saddest part was true
No one could ever love you
You'll end up thrown away.
Disposed. In an alley
Where nobody knows.

I often wonder
As an older Father
To two young boys
Whether I will have
The time left to see
Them grown up and maybe
Even have their own

Little families and careers.
I want to be that old fart
Sitting in the garden
With my Grandchildren
Climbing all over my ruined,
Aged, old body and hearing
It creak like an old floorboard
Knowing that my dinner
Is being prepared for me
And there is wine in the fridge.
I long for that opportunity
To share with my boys
So that I know before
I finally leave them
I will have left them in good hands
With a great future
Ahead of them. It's the very
Last gift I'll work towards giving them.

I like the taste
And the side effects
Of alcohol too much
To quit it even though
I know it is slowly
Killing me like it did
With three of my brothers.
However it helps me
With my creativity
And the nightmares
I suffer from every night.
I wake up each morning
Promising myself away
From the poison but like
A death deal gone wrong
I sit alone again drowning
My body with this shit
That only has one objective.

You never smile
At me anymore
And it saddens me
That this is all we've
Become. We became
Strangers and don't even
Have the energy
To acknowledge each other
Anymore. We tick days off
From the calendar
As we have nothing left
To look forward too
Except avoiding each other
And playing parents
To two unsuspecting kids.
Not aware of the imminent
Disaster that we've set
Ourselves and them up for.

In our quest we usually
Have to suffer many defeats
Before we can raise ourselves
Back to our feet again.
It is normal. It is everyday life.
Be nice to those people
Who you collude with on
Your way up as they will
Still be there waiting for you
On your way down.
Be humble. Be appreciative
Of your surroundings
As one day it could all be over
And then you're the one
At the bottom of the ladder
Looking up as life passes you by.

You became a walking
Meth lab. An amphetamine
Whore who skipped through
Life and fell through doors
And no saving grace
Could ever hide the trace
Of that lost little girl inside
Lost and distant and outta space.
You had blown up lips
That could no longer kiss
And the saddest part was true
No one could ever love you.
You'll end up thrown away.
Disposed. In an alley where
Nobody even knows.

The party ended
And you returned home.
Defeated. Alone and
Out of pocket.
You picked up the tab
At the bar yet it
Impressed no one.
You got some smiles
A few fake numbers
That you desperately
Tried to send messages too.
But this blurred, drunken
Version of you was
Already on the road to ruin
And nobody wanted to
Connect with you
Only to be dragged down
Under the currents
And into the abyss.
A place you knew so well
But denied all knowledge of.

She was the desert Queen
Yet hid in the shadows
Away from the wolves
And coyotes set out to attack
Always. She would sit alone
In the Badlands wondering
About the crumbling empire
She ruled and watch the sun
Go down. Her throne room
Was a cave and her soldiers,
Tired old men. Hungry and
Beaten down by life.
She knew that the time had
Come and heard the armies
Approaching from the east.
She smiled one last time
As she plunged the knife
Into her own heart.
These were troubled times for some.

You're never too
Old to dream.
It's only when
You stop dreaming
That you become old
And at that point
Time has already
Ran out!

The passion fizzles out
Of you the older you get
As your outlook on life
In general shifts through
Every experience and
Encounter you've been
Put through. You become
Wary of others and trust

Less than when you were
Younger as there is normally
An ulterior motive to
Kindness these days.
Every random act comes
With a price tag to it
Or a slice of your soul
In advance. So you guard
Yourself all the time
And in that act you may have
Lost an opportunity
Or avoided a debt
That will hang over you
For the rest of your life.

It was that desire
I had held onto
For a life time to
See you both again
A Fathers loss
Which never helped my pain
It has been so long
I feel ashamed
But it was never my choice
I didn't write the rules
To this game.
I saw a photo of how
You are both now
That broke my heart
And drained my power
I just wanted to see you
If only for an hour
But I can't even hold a photo
All our memories devoured.

As I looked out
Of my upper windows
And listened to the
Howling wind smashing
Against anything it could find
I found myself feeling jealous
Of the freedom that it had
To go and do absolutely
Anything it wanted.
I wanted to open my window
And jump up into the loam
And fly away from this place.
I wanted that separation
To journey among the Gods
And become at one
With this beautiful planet
We inhabit.

I have more to offer
To those who actually
Want to know me
As oppose to those
In life that spend
Every living moment
Trying to exploit
My kindness and naivety.
You see, my biggest
Weakness has always
Been trust and generosity.
Time and time again
This has turned out to be
My biggest achilles heel
And the end result
Is always an empty
Bank account, a broken heart
And even less trust
In the people that surround me.

Just spent the day
Reading fake reviews
On my books on Amazon
From someone I deleted
From Facebook for being
A complete fantasist
And fraud and it made
Me smile. After all he was
Not a verified purchaser
And my 6 year old has
A better understanding
Of talent and the English
Language than this douchebag.
Tonight I continued writing
Book number five and laughed
To myself as I looked at
My growing CV. I feel sorry
For him. Maybe I should
Share some of my royalties
With him to help him buy
A new kitchen table
That is apparently being
Propped up by my first book
Or an education.

I felt the heat rising
And the pressure was on.
You wanted a masterpiece
But you gave me no time
At all to prepare for
Something that we'd
Both only make pennies on.
We sat in a bar eating
Sushi and drinking warm Sake
While watching the
Street freaks stumble past

Us both like a punch
In the face. We had to do
Something different
Or tomorrow we are going
To hire a trailer to take
This old cash cow to auction.
We needed a new resource
And I was the sacrifice.

It got to the stage
Where I'd absolutely
Ran out of ideas
And inspiration.
Yet all I wanted
To do was write.
I spent my whole life
Dreaming of becoming
A Poet and was happy
To not make a penny
From it. So I gave everything
To the craft. I'm at that stage
Now where my worst enemy
Has come back again
To ground me. He is called
Writers block and he
Shows no remorse.
And once again as an artist
And a writer I am again
Out of words and back
On skid row with this
Shadow once again
Looming over me as I look
For another way out.

The day had been long
And with little reward.
I sat on the last train home

And could just feel
The energy drained from
My broken body.
I wanted to watch
An old movie and sip
On a bourbon with coke
And ice and chew on a rack
Of ribs. I wanted to sit
In the dark with just the
Glow of candles and the silence
Of my house at midnight.
Only the gentle snoring
Of my children upstairs
Fast asleep helped my mood.
I knew that I'd see them
In the morning and that
Made everything immediately
Better.

I looked to you
In my darkest hour
But found no light.
How I miss our old
Conversations and banter.
I miss the silly messages
And playing football
Even though I always lost.
In fact, I just miss
Absolutely everything
About you.
You were my older brother.
My idol. My hero.
My very best friend.
And I miss you so much
Even though I cannot bear
To grieve for you.
It's not that I don't want too

It's just that if I do
I am scared that I'll never stop
Grieving and I will go
Off the rails.
I'm sad that my boys
Will never get to meet you
Wayne. I am sad that I will
Never see you ever again.

I'd hide behind my curtains
And watch the world pass by
I smile although I'm feeling sad
As tears flow from my eyes
I'd speak to friends
And read for a while
Pretend that it's not true
But life has taught me well
Yet there's a demon in my view.

Some people are like furniture
They just sit there
Do absolutely nothing
Gather dust
And then get replaced
For something better.

View everyone
With suspicion
As you will
Never really know
Their agenda
Until it is
Too late.

Our minds
Are oceans.
The deeper
We discover
The deeper
We learn.

I truly believe
That we all have
Our own calling
And that each one
Of us are here to
Serve a purpose.
I had my true calling
Just over a year ago.
I was put here to
Put words together
And publish books
Of prose and poetry.
I look at each of my
Children and wonder
What theirs will be
And whether I will
Be around to see it.

You led me
To the slaughter
Like a horse
To water
And my final
Memories of you
Was the dead look
In your eyes
As you watched
Me falling over the edge.
This maelstrom
And chaos now over.

You set me free.
Finally.

I lay down alone
On the couch and enjoy
The coldness and solitude.
The birds sing a pretty song
Which announces the start
Of a new day. The darkness
I lay in seems peaceful
As the chaos that ensues
Is yet to penetrate my soul.
Alone here I feel relaxed.
Almost in a Zen like state
Of consciousness.
The sun yet to rise and
It's 5am somewhere.

Today I woke up
In total silence and peace
And only the darkness of
The morning and the
Coolness of my couch
Were all that mattered
In those lean, sweet hours.
It was my 43rd birthday
And although I would
Spend the whole day
And night at work
I would still not have to
Spend it alone. I wanted a
Cake with candles. Something
My boys could blow out.
Instead I got my request
For the day off denied.
While outside the sun started
To shine brightly and the birds

Sang to me. It was the 8th May 2018.
I had made it through
Another year. Unscathed. For now.

Tear yourself open
Show your pain
To all of the haters
And to those who
Will never know what
It is like to struggle.
Keep them safe
In their ivory towers
While the monster
In me wants to burn
It to the ground.

Take teachings from me
And I will guide you
Through your route along life.
Invest time in me
And I will nurture you
And harness the greatness
That is inside of you
But currently asleep.
Unknown potential.
Take the knowledge I have
Taken the time to learn
And use it to enhance
Your own library.
Make you mind the best book
Anyone will ever read
As we all sparkle inside.

Send me naked
Pictures of yourself.
I am an artist
And I need to know

What I'll be working with.

I watch you as you sleep
The calmness and peace
Set deep on your handsome face.
You make me proud.
Oh so proud.
You are the baby
Of our little family yet
Seem old beyond your
Two years. Has it only been
Such a short time together
As it seems like I've known you
My whole life Carter.
I think of everything we must do
Before I depart and it makes me
Realise that I have to hold out
For as long as I can
So I can enjoy you
For as long as I can.

Decide what kind
Of shit you want
To post out for people
To criticize.
After all, whatever
You post, everyone is
The next Charles Bukowski,
Dylan Thomas or Baudelaire.
Pour a Mohito
Open some Tacos
And fry some mince.
Celebrate another culture.
Enjoy the amazing food
After all, it's an education
And we leave
With our stomachs full.

These are the things
We always sought after
When we could no longer
Write in block capitals
Because we were too drunk!

I've not written recently.
You see, I've been afraid
To share what I think
At times like this and my
Impending refusal to accept
Stupidity always gets me
In trouble. It seems that
Everyone is a critic and
Everyone is insulted
By the truth therefore
It's best to stay quiet sometimes.

If you write poetry
And chose to
Show it to no one
Then when you die
It gets lost in translation
And your legacy
Has been lost.
What a waste of
A talent that could
Have been a catalyst
For this next
Generation of writers.
You've betrayed your art
And the people
Who love it.

She said
Come to me
And together
We can create
A beautiful madness
That will drive
Us both insane.

Me at 23:13pm isn't
Something flattering.
Working that mirror
I saw all of my flaws.
The effects of 43 years
If a very tough life
Staring back at me
Accusatory.
I saw the grey hair
The lines under my eyes.
I looked tired but inside
I felt young still.
The worst part of growing
Old is that it is a process
The heart fights
But the body taps out to.

Life only became
Difficult because the
Need to spend
Our whole day
In a death grip
With our smart phones
Stuck to our hands
Pumping out duck faced
Selfies with stupid eyebrows
Painted on people's faces.
You made a really
Bad job seem relevant.

You told me that
Me and you would be
The eater of worlds
But when the battle
Came into town
The witnesses to the
Killings were already
Out the door and on
Their way home.

Ian Curtis
One day you
And I will
Compare words
In another
World far, far
From here
Where only the
Angels dwell
And the music
Is always played
Loudly.

The watery stare
Of a drunks eye
Follows you around
The room waiting for you
To rest your glass
So he can seize his moment.
He sits in the corner
Coiled like a serpent
Ready to strike and steal
Another meal for free.

She said
Come to me
And together
We can create
A beautiful madness
That will drive
Us both insane.

The stories we make
Up through our
Lifetimes are told
Solely by us for an
Audience of many.
It is our experiences
That we add to our
Very own portfolios
That shape the personalities
That we sculpt and perfect.
And it is this that makes
Us attractive to others
Not just our appearance.

I was generally
The first name on
The team shift
But as I grew older
The opportunities
Passed over to younger
Players with less
Experience. I sat on
The bench and watched
The team I loved lose
Week after week
And it hurt as I knew
That I could make
A real difference.
Eventually we were

Relegated with the same
Group of kids the manager
Put his faith in.
They were offered
New contracts to stay
And underachieve again.
I was released.

Icing sugar coated
Turkish Delight with
Ice cold Riesling wine
And a beautiful sunset
In a 70 degree evening.
The Sahara loomed
Over the horizon
And the smells of
Spices and freshly made
Bread made my mouth
Water all the more.
I read Hemingway and
Chewed on ripe figs and
Listened to local musicians
Playing late into the night
While children slept
Under the stars and dreamt.
I could never feel at peace
Like this ever again.
If I died tonight
My life would have been
Worth something after all.

The hardest thing
In the world is
To say goodbye.
It's almost time
Now and I'm at peace
With myself.

I wonder how many
Of those who follow me
Actually follow me
And my life.
Read my words.
Purchased my books.
We amass a lot of
Human traffic during
Our lives. We share
Absolutely everything.
We strip ourselves bare.
Exposed always.
Some ask for more
Than they are expected
To give but offer nothing
In return. I'm at the age now
Where all I have is
This notepad and ink pen.
I want to share the
Very best bits.
I want to be remembered.

I wanted to exercise
My demons but after
Two bottles of white
French wine and steak
With oyster starters
And a vanilla froth
I just wanted to sit down
And listen to Beethoven
And watch a movie.
We race along in our youth
Hot our thirties and then
Plan ahead eventually.
Once we hit our forties
All bets are off.
We watch our children

Growing older and
All we want to do
Is stay alive long enough
To make sure that
We can enjoy what is
Left of our time together.

I once lived
In Paris
But she fell
To earth and utterly
Out of love
With me.
My lifestyle
Mad her mad.
Her head hurt
In the morning.
She finally got bored
Of the constant
Hangover and her
Credit card
Being declined.
I left with a shadow
Over me. I never returned.

We stand here
In the asylum
Watching as all
Of the lunatics
Are set free.
Back into the world
That rejected them
In the first place
And wonder where
They go from here.

We shared thoughts
From the prisons
Of our minds
Only to be ignored
And left confused
By it all. It was meant
To get easier the older
We got but somehow
Everything became
More difficult to sustain.
We became reclusive
And stunted in our knowledge
And hid behind closed doors.
We thought we were
Living the dream
But then we awoke.

Cherry pie
Apple pie
Moonshine.
Started tonight
By drinking
Sauvignon Blanc.
Wanted to watch
A movie but have
A child that refuses
To fall asleep.
I tried a lullaby
While the cat pawed
At me like a pin cushion.
I have the school run
To do tomorrow morning
As a reward for finally
Getting a day off.
Relaxation always comes
With a price and bad service.
Think I need a refund.

It was a long night
That ended the next
Morning. I woke up with
My head in intensive care
While using a Jim Morrison
Poster as a blanket.
The girl in the corner glared
At me with crazed eyes
And a mad soul. I offered to
Sleep on the floor
And she accepted.
She fell asleep with
Jim Morrison and tore his heart
In two as she slept.
I woke up devastated.
I needed a new poster
For my wall.

The Moonshine
In a fancy jar
Sold legally at
Supermarkets across
The U.K looks great
Until you chill it
And serve it over ice
With ginger ale.
I wanted to experience
Something similar
However I went to bed
With a taste in my mouth
Like I kissed a frog
Chewing on wallpaper
Paste. I woke up with a
Bad feeling that my whole
Day on the toilet
Would never end.

Hard to switch off
When you are
Consistently
Switched on.
The body clock
Stuck on a different
Vibe to the world
Around it, and we
Wonder why we spend
So much time
Chasing our tails.

It was a novel idea
To write a novel
My dear, but remained
Definitely clear
Was the need to
Disappear. To find a
Way clear of the
Pain around here
As you whisper
In my ear there is
More to life than fear.

I came to you
A broken soul
Looking for a way out
But instead you
Repaired me
And gave me a way
Back in again.
You taught me that
Each day was a blessing
So many of us take
For granted. I no longer
Pray for each day to end
Rather for it to begin.

I find it visually
More attractive
Writing in other
Languages rather
Than my own.
Somehow the words
Look prettier,
More elegant and
Sound better
On the tongue.
We make it an art.
Through this we
Create our own magic.

(Same poem in French below):

Je le trouve visuellement
Plus attractif
Ecriture dans d'autres
Langues plutot
Que la mienne.
En quelque sorte les mots
Look plus joli,
Plus elegante et
Ca sonne mieux sur la langue.
Nous en faisons un art.
Grace a cela, nous
Creer notre proper magie.

How many words get lost
Along the way.
How many glances
Between you and I
Over the years have now
Become frowns?
How many times
Do I stay away.

Because the truth is
Our worst nightmare
And nobody loves you
When you're down and out.

She told me that
I'd be the perfect
Lover if I savored
Her body the way
I savor my glasses
Of wine. In response
I told her it was medicinal
And her love was
Unconditional. I poured
Another glass and told
Her everything would
Be fine.

I woke up
With 4 hours
On the clock
And a busy
Bank Holiday
Monday due.
I want to drink wine
And sing country music
By Johnny Cash
Or Willy Nelson.
The night is clammy
And sweaty.
Plus the baby won't sleep.
My work friend
Will not stop calling me.
I'm in the bath
She's calling me.
I'm cooking pasta
In my guy pants,

She's calling me.
She wants to sell me
An apology she doesn't own.
I silence my phone
Look at the fucking thing
And shake my head
At how fragile
Technology has made us.
She's picking me up
In a few hours.
I look forward to
Annoying her with
My views on her musical
Taste and my early
Morning aftershave.
Tomorrow I will wear
Eternity by Calvin Klien.
From the sounds of it
Tomorrow will last for
Eternity also. We will do
Coffee & breakfast together.
I'll pick up the cheque.

Sifting through memories
From my think tank
And I realized that every one
That we had together
Was a passing moment
And not anything you
Could construe as a
Planned meeting.
It made me realise
Just how little time
We actually spent together
And now realise why
We will never get
Those moments back.

Life moved on
And so did we without
A backward glance
At one another.

As Ian Curtis
Once sang
Love will tear
Us apart again.
It will.
It always does.
There's no
Copywriter on
This one. It's a lyric
From someone
Long dead
Who hung from
A room like a
Magpie flies through
The skies. I'm no visitor
To the pain.
My older brother
Did it too.
I'm the survivor.

We strive
In a difficult life
To survive
Yet the linear
That lines us
In our moments
Of need fall apart
At the seams
And we are left
Stranded in the oceans
And valleys
Of lost dreams.

It suddenly dawned
On me that you'd never
Even walked a mile
In my shoes yet we're
Always too quick to
Criticize at every
Opportunity. It made me
Feel sorry for the kind
Of person that you were.
You were terribly weak
Minded and all I wanted
To do was laugh in the face
Of your ignorance.
But instead I extended out
My hand and offered you
Friendship. It was all
I could do.

Born free without
The credit made available
To us in later years
That ends up crippling us.
We thought life would
Be so much easier as adults
But realized with age comes
Responsibilities that end up
Dragging us under the waves
And drowns us. Only the salty
Taste in our mouths as we
Sink deeper into the abyss
Comes for free. It is the last
Drink we will ever savour
And finally the world ends
With us becoming a marine community.
Sent back to the watery fibres
Of the womb one last time
To start the cycle all over again.

Hold onto every
Relationship you have
And show it the
Love and respect
It deserves. Share that smile.
Kiss goodnight. Say hello.
Wave goodbye. Never take
Any moment together
For granted. Even if it's a
Bad one. An argument is
Easily overturned. Look at
What you've earnt and
Be grateful that you've
Got this far. It's a journey
Some never see through
To the end.

You drank me
Like a milkshake
And thanked me
For the nutrients.
You said the body
Was a greedy
Machine that always
Needed feeding
And that next time
We should put this
Elixir somewhere else.
You had a part of
Your body that could
Make us a baby.

I will never
Understand
The four lined poet.
There are no
Foundations

To a quote.
Make the speech
Longer otherwise
The audience will
Soon get bored
And leave the arena.

Sneeze on me
Spit on me
Lick me clean.
I want to taste
Every part
And smell.
Every scent
That belongs
To you.
Share your body
With me always
As you belong
To me.

Your words will
Lose their power
If you over dilute
Them. You can write
A thousand poems
But if they all read
Like the last one
It is time to put
The pen down and
Take a timeout.
The mind is like
A computer that can
Sometimes create
Its own virus.
Be careful yours
Doesn't get hacked.

Those unlucky enough
To have never experienced
Parenthood, through the
Highs and lows and sleepless
Nights, have never truly
Experienced how diverse
And beautiful life really is.
I woke up to two pairs
Of crystal blue eyes and
Handsome smiling faces
Gazing at me, and all I
Saw on their features
Was the look of pure love.
It made me realise just
How lucky I really am.

One day these eyes
Will close for
A final time
And everything
They've experienced
Will be lost forever.

I hate the fact
That I have to get
Drunk these days
To put up with you.
It takes that edge away
From my personality.
The one you've tried
So hard to destroy.
Maybe you were jealous.
Maybe you needed control.
Either way, I'm not a
Remote control toy.
You cannot control me.
I was a person before

I met you and I will be
A person again one day
Once I've found the key
To this jail cell
That you keep me in.

I set fire to myself.
I tried to burn away
All of the bad stuff
That life threw at me.
After a while I realized
That it wasn't me
That was on fire
More so my surroundings.
I was in Hell
And I was burning
For my sins.

Sometimes I sit alone
In the garden
When the weather permits
And I think about you.
I shed a tear for only
Myself as I have never
Openly grieved for the three
Lost boys in my life.
I smell the sandlewood
Watch the acorns drop
Missing my head by inches.
I sip expensive wine
And dread the thought
Of my own two little boys
Ever losing each other
And wonder how they
Would cope if it ever
Happened, which one day
It will. There's a cool breeze

Tonight like a kiss
From an absent friend.
It left me with a smile
Maybe I even blushed.

I threw a pebble
Into a small brook.
It didn't skim across
The water like a
Shape shifter.
It sank. I placed my
Hopes on that solitary
Pebble crossing over.
Somehow it represented me
As it sank. So did I.
I felt let down and once
Again I felt short changed.
I backed no winners
And lost a weeks worth
Of beer money on a loser
And now I'd better go
And clear my bar tab.
It's almost closing time.

I want to write
Real poetry with
Real poets. Collaborate.
Make an amazing product.
Take back our world
From the zombie phone
Era. The baggy trouser
Bum boy brigade.
I want to sit in a silent
Room with a candle,
The purring of my pussy's
(feline, not feminine).
I could never afford

A harem and just write.
I want to eat pizza
Under the stars while the
Sounds of next doors
Waterfall soothes my soul.
I want some get up and go
I want to lose control.

Your ghost visits me
Each night. I suffer from
Sleep psychosis. That feeling
Of being pinned to the bed
And the white noise
Is unbearable. The smell
Of Sulphur, the images.
I can almost hear the song
Mad World by Tears For Fears.
I see a Jason mask
A Kruger knife glove
A red balloon floating
And the chuckle of child
Sized dolls with sharp knives
And demonic eyes.
In a hot sweat, I ran outside
Into the rain and washed my soul
From the juices of Mother Nature.
I drowned in the beauty
Of her sin, but like a child
Sucking from the nipple
I was well fed and swam
Into the darkness of a dream.

I was never
My own biggest fan
But if I was drowning
And I held out my hand
Would you save me?

I could punch
Myself in the face
Repeatedly and still
Never be satisfied
With the pain that
I would love to inflict
On myself for the life
I have lived and the life
I still do. I see myself as
A 43 year old Peter Pan.
One day I will need to
Grow up. Life doesn't allow
You to be a child forever.

You're a Doctor
Healing broken hearts
Help mine as it's
Falling completely apart.

The pain we contain
Is sustainable
But we choose to keep
It locked away.
If we can't remember it
Then it never really
Existed in the first place.

We kill a horror
Story with a lie.
The second we hit
Our beds we already know
What is waiting underneath it.
With a smile and a greedy
Chuckle, the paint smears
From it's face and the balloons
Start to rise from the floorboards.
The carousel music begins

It's time for the circus
To hit the town.

Andy Warhol
Once said that
Everyone would be
Famous for 15 minutes.
Share your moments
With the world.

I sat up until 4am
When I knew that
The wine had ran out
And all of my hundreds
Of Facebook "friends"
Had gone to sleep
And researched those
I shared my closest
Memories and photos with.
I found it amusing
How many people had
Actually silently
Deleted me, yet still smile
At me daily at work
Thinking I hadn't noticed?

A Campari and
Lemonade. I sat in
A 1980's bar in Soho
Watching all the posh boys
Mince around acting queer.
Fake smiles and fake love
For one another. Smiling at
Each other but looking at
The person behind them.
I was the one straight man
In a suit at the bar.

Wrong time, wrong place.
I held the joker card.
My dinner buddy was
My 6.5 foot black man
Bestie – gay and married.
I asked him to drop his pants
To scare them away.
I almost fainted!

Being made to watch
Masha and the Bear
Continuously on my day
Off wasn't what I had
In mind. So instead
I tune off wearing jjust
My Joy Division T-Shirt
And boxer shorts while
Drinking ginger and lemon
Tea and eating hot toast.
The housework is done
The sun shines outside.
I pick up my pen and write
While my youngest
Chills on his sofa.
These lean, sweet moments
Together are absolutely
Priceless.

This hunger inside us
Is driven by the desire
To always be the very
Best that we can.
For is we did not have
This focus then everything
Around us would be
Out of reach.
We would have no

Goals to aim for.
Our lives would become
Monotonous and we'd
Forever carry this envy
Towards others that would
Eventually tear us apart.
Failure is not an option.
Always play to win.
Life is a short game
That sometimes ends too soon.

I scrunch
My hands
Into my belly.
Feels like kneading
Dough and I wish that
I had a plan to return
This body back to
It's original owner
In better condition.

It got harder
To love you and
It hurt like hell
Watching something
That was once
Beautiful die.
It hurt more pretending
That it could still work
When clearly it was
Already over. Every day
Going through the
Rigmarole and going
To bed miserable.
After a while I was glad
That you found someone else.
It finally freed me

From that prison cell
I called my life.
Now go on and play
Someone else's jailor.

Me.
Me.
Me.
I have a
Narcissistic
Personality
And all I
Ever think
About
Is myself.

When I'm finally dead
I don't want to be shown
To those who grieve
For me dressed in an
Immaculate suit and tie.
I want to be laid out
Naked. Just so those
I left behind can see
The damage that
My addiction did to my
Body in the hope that
My death and denial
Could possibly awaken
Someone to save a life.

Look Heavenward
And remember that
They still watch over us
And that we will always
Be loved by those who left
Us behind in their passing.

All I ever wanted
To be was myself
And even that
Became so hard for me.
It got to the point
Where I stopped
Knowing myself anymore.
I became a ghost
Of the man I struggled
To become.
The smell of death
Hung around me
Like an aftershave.
I dated alcohol as she
Was my one consistent
Companion. But she was
A greedy lover that would
End up taking everything
Away from me.
Including my life.

For her it was
A moment of magic
For him ejaculation.
He rolled off his
Teenage lover and
Got dressed.
He made his excuses
And left. What he left
Behind slowly ran down
Her left thigh.
She laid alone
Feeling cheap and confused
While he moved on
To his next 'fix'.

Citronella candle
And dinner for two
With my youngest.
I was tucking into Pimms
And steak, he had chips
And chicken with an OJ.
I sat there under the sun
Feeling like the whole
Journey was made
For moments
Just like this one.

We sit in the
Cheap seats
Drinking $5 bourbon
And eating chili dogs
While cheering on
A horse that has no
Chance of leaving
The track with its life
Let alone the prize money.
We live a five & dime
Life in rented rooms
East / West of Michigan
And wonder how we ended
Up so far away from
The Sunset Strip.
All those years studying
Taught us nothing about
The life we would eventually
End up with. We checked
Our grade papers
And felt cheated.

The words rolled
Off her tongue
With the velvet sheen
Of a mystery. She called
Herself the Queen of L.A
But I could see straight
Through her façade.
She sat there in fake
Leather jeans and a
Killer smile. She just
Looked straight through me
And before I knew what
Was happening
She was driving me
Back to whatever
Hell she came from.

We get to an age
When we find
A new found respect
For our childhood
Comfort blanket
And a wish for
It's return.

The rain pours down
We watch from inside
As the windows protect
Us from the fury of
Nature. Still the sun
Is shining in
The background.
I think we're going to
See a rainbow
Around the next corner.

As much as I love
My moments alone
I crave the cuddles
From my two beautiful
Sons. The roads are sealed
With gold but without them
I am only treading
Muddy waters.
I struggle through
The tide just to be
With them again.

You drive through
Stormy clouds everyday
Survive long shifts
Bad decisions
From incompetent
Managers who swim
Against the tide
With no plans to reach
The shore. They float
Always and hope they
Find a piece of driftwood
And make it in one piece.
Awoken with sand
In their hair and a salty
Taste in their mouths
They stand in line
And act like this was all
A part of their plan.
In essence they survived
The storm. The rest of us
Called for a taxi for those
Who wanted to travel
On our success.
We left the rest behind
At the station.

In our team we don't
Carry any passengers.

We choose rhyme
Over reason and
Wonder why we turn
Up to work with a
Song stuck in our heads
For the rest of the day.
It's Sunday morning.
7am early. My body
Has decided that after
A long week I only
Needed four hours sleep
On my one day off.
The mind hums like
A machine that was
Just turned on and
Tuned in. My babies asleep.
The cats sleep. The world
Sleeps. Even the birds
Outside sleep. I know this
Through their lack of song.
But I? I never sleep!
Even when I die
Somehow and eye
Will slowly open and
Continue to mock me
For eternity.

Inside every
Personality
Is a fragility
That splinters
Each time it's exposed.
She said sex sold
On the streets

But was happy
Just to give it away.

The real world sleeps
As the fake world
Decides who they
Are going to be
Tomorrow.

She looked like she
Was worth a million
Dollars but you could
Tell that she was just
Another wannabe
Sunset Queen.
She had sores around
Her mouth and smelt
Like last night's bar action.
She was never going to
Find the right punter.
She was death in a glass.
She glanced back
As she walked in front
Of the rail car.
We could all see this
Happening yet nobody
Cared enough to save her.

I watch the boys
Eat their spaghetti
And then afterwards
Sliced strawberries.
I sit writing and indulge
In a cold white wine
While the sounds of
Gary Numan's Telekon
Album makes up the

Background noise.
It's currently competing
With a cartoon but
All I can hear is the
Sounds of the dark 1980's
Synth pop era.
Strangely I feel relaxed.

It is no surprise
That all men are
Drawn to a females
Chest. After all
We exited from a
Vagina and our
Very first meal was
From a breast.
Mothers milk.
At that stage
In our lives
Cows did not exist
So we drank the
Elixir from the Gods
And grew strong.

I looked out towards
The cherry blossom trees
And the sun came out
To give the day
Its shine back.
I felt worn out
Yet still had a fire
Burning inside of me.
I grow older yet the
Wisdom is something
That keeps us younger.
I decided on lobster
And champagne for lunch.

It was my day off
After all. I sat there
In the garden and took
A moment to appreciate
Everything I had at
That moment in time.
Tomorrow the struggle
Begins again. I will be ready.

Apparently
These days
Someone
Can write
Three words
And get
A thousand
Likes?
Publish a book
Of four lined
Poetry
And make a
Publishing house.
Clearly I am
Doing something
Wrong?
I write a book
And fill each page.
Apparently that's called
Over feeding people?

I bid you all goodnight.
Today was hard.
A colleague made me
Smile. He called me posh?
I see myself as a
Toilet roll.
The World Cup

Started.
Men came back home
From their five & dime
Jobs with a bag of beer
And a tired home sitter.
She cooked pasta.
He wanted caviar.
This was no new romance.
Wasn't meant to last
Past the group stages.
Let's hope we don't
Get eliminated early on.

Hate is a cancer
That spreads throughout
Your entire body
And destroys whatever
Decent is left inside
Of you. Find that cure.
Call a Doctor.
Make peace with
Yourself and start
The healing process.

I'm assuming that
I will sell more of
My books once I am
No longer alive
But for now I live
For the art I produce
While my phone shows
An unknown caller
Trying to infiltrate
My quiet time.

You walked from
The scene of the crash.
Mist surrounded you.
My phone had died.
I wanted to run
But was drawn by your aura.
You walked straight
Past me in silence.
The smell of rose water
And sadness lingered.
I turned around to call
Out to you
But your ghost
Had disappeared.

We no longer
Pick up a book
And spend a time out
Immersed in that world.
It seems like my
Eyesight is failing
And all I do is write
While the page
Looks fuzzy.
Are these those small
Telltale signs
When your secret is over.
I got an appointment
With an eye guy.
My face doesn't need
Another addition.

Love dies
And the fallout
Is immense.
Try sharing a bed
With someone
You can't even
Say goodnight to
As you roll over to sleep.

Pitch your sales
For the new
Audience.
Everyone's a sucker
For a cheap idea
These days.

I want to spend
Some time writing
A decent poem
And drink a lot of wine.
Later on a Keith Floyd
Cooking show from the 1980's.
I love the nostalgia
And passion the old school
TV Chefs had especially as
To them it was all about
The art and not the fame.

Crossing the road
And watching the
Elderly couple
Holding hands
Always raises a smile
For I know not many
Relationships last as
Long as they used to.
The world was simpler

Back then and people
Actually interacted
With one another.
They sat down and spoke
Without the technology
We have these days
When all we can do I look
Into a phone and wear
Our trousers falling from our asses.

This constant need
To reproduce Human
Beings must be tiring
And time consuming.
Just walked past a Lady
With six children this morning
On the school run
And wondered what
She does in her spare time?

We meander in our
Soulless existence and
Only the silence and
Lack of knowledge
Towards life gains us that
Edge that keeps us alive.
We study science.
Travel to space.
Walk on the moon.
All of a sudden
We've become the aliens.

If life was any
Machine of my choice
It would be a car
With only one gear.
Reverse!

Many of us will
Never meet each
Other or share a
Moment together.
Yet before we die
We will know more
About each other
Than we do ourselves.
We will laugh together
Cry together yet
Will only rely on
What the other has
Posted on their digital profile.

Fighting with Angels
Dancing with Devils.
We are always fighting
Between good and evil.
We constantly swim
Against the tide with
Serpent fingers clutching
At our heels and wild
Horses kicking among the waves.
We slip into a chlorine dream
And sink slowly down
Into our salty graves.

David Bowie
Was a God to me.
I need to find
Another world
Where I may one day
Find my Starman
Again. Major Tom,
Can you still
Hear me?

The worms eat away
At what little we left
Behind. They show no respect
For who we once were.
Be it homeless or political
Warlords. We all share the
Same fate eventually
And the food chain shows
Us absolutely no respect
Whatsoever. There is solitude
In our final hour.
The body is a vessel.
It only holds our appearance.
And so I sit and wonder.
Where does the spirit go?

Each person moves
Through that revolving
Door. Never to be seen
Again. Never to be
Remembered by us at all.
We wait for others
To walk back into
Our lives. We wait for
Those who have departed
To make contact.
Some kind of signal.
We spend our whole lives
Waiting for something
To happened instead of
Making it happen.
We wait for death knowing
That is the one thing
That we can never outrun.

The beauty faded
And we were left
With just a glimmer
Of hope.
The angel dust
Faded and all
We were left with
Was the remains
Of a someone
Who could have been
Anyone she ever wanted.
Politics pay a price
If you choose to
Gamble in vice.

I woke up
Still drunk.
Mouth like
Sandpaper
And the smell
In the room
Was insane.
I rolled over
To see a death glare.
I didn't remember
Bringing her home
Or how the night
Panned out.
Guess now I do.

We swim with the tide
Like dead fish
And wonder why
We get lost through
The channels.
There's an ocean
Out there and we become

A part of the food chain.
We sail like a ghost ship
With no direction.
Greedy currents pull
Us under and we become
Yet another ship wreck.

She dances with
Diamonds in her hair.
Her smile is a torn
Piece of flesh and her
Wild eyes burn like fire.
She has a dangerous
Beauty you dare not
Admire. She whispers
In your ears. She is a
Train wreck. Hardwired.

I love the way
That your eyes smile.
I can see your soul
Shining from inside.
Making people delirious.
Fireworks. A kaleidoscope.
You were born to make
The magic that life craves.
I saw you as an equal
But in reality I would
Always be inferior to you.

I sometimes wonder
Whether or not
If you would reach out
A hand and pull me
From the abyss.
Would you watch me
Drown. Slowly sinking

Down into a salty grave.
My watery journey
Back into the womb
Of the world.
I saw you smile
As you walked away
Knowing that it was
Never your intention
To see me again.

When sadness
Is all that you have
Left in your heart
And you wonder why
It wasn't you
And why you are still here.
The lump in your throat
That you will swallow
And you feel sorry
For yourself as a default
Sign. A young Lady at work
Got diagnosed with
Cancer and I laid
On the sofa at 3am
With a tear in my eye
Watching my baby sleep
And wondering how her
Parents feel right now.
I admire her strength
And her dignity.
I want to get to know her better
And give her a hug.
I want to do more than
Just smile and say Hi!

The rain pours down
We watch from inside
As the windows protect
Us from the fury of
Nature. Still the sun
Is shining in the background.
I think we're going to
See a rainbow
Around the next corner.

As much as I love
My moments alone
I crave the cuddles
I get from my two
Beautiful Sons. The roads
Are sealed with gold
But without them
I am only treading
Stormy waters.
I struggle through
The tide just to be
With them again.

Is there a life
On Mars?
David, I will find
You there.
I only wanted
An autograph.

$16 for a 46 paged
Book of poetry?
I'd rather call it a
Pamphlet and save my
Money. At what stage
Do people think that
Putting up a book

With a lack of content
Was going to be
Acceptable? At what point
Did they think they'd
Make a career out
Of this? I was watching
The 2018 World Cup
With a glass of cold wine.
Black and white cat
Called Fucker by my side.
I found this art so simple
To perfect.

We kiss goodbye to
The project and open
Up the chapter to
Something entirely new.
This was never the
Direction I planned
For in the beginning
And now feel like I've
Made a short cut.

Acknowledgements:

Every books takes a lot out of you and you wonder sometimes if you will ever end it, and this book has been no different. There was an accident a few weeks back and my laptop was damaged, the hard drive gone and this book would never had seen the day of light if not for an old friend of mine and computer God, James Norbury. He managed to somehow recover this book that I honestly thought was lost, and will be forever in his debt.

We meet a lot of people on our journey, and some are people that you rarely see, but are always there for you at the drop of a hat. James is one of these guys alongside his Wife Becky & Daughter Keely. Thank you so much and the first copy goes out to you.

Book Six started. I will spend the rest of the year on this next one so if you want sneak previews, check out my Facebook Authors page.

Live well, Love often. Be at peace and enjoy the ride.

John Davies 10/07/2018.